To everyone who dares to dream and strives to grow—may you find the courage within to embrace your true potential. This book is for you, the seekers of strength and the architects of your destiny.

DREAM DARE DO

"BE BOLD , BE COURAGEOUS, AND MAKE YOUR PASSION A REALITY!!!"

BHAVESH POOJARI

Contents

Contents

Foreword

In a world where doubt often overshadows our aspirations, the journey to confidence can feel like an uphill battle. Yet, it is a journey worth embarking on, as the path to personal development not only transforms our own lives but also inspires those around us.

This book is a beacon for anyone seeking to unlock their potential and cultivate a mindset of self-belief. Within these pages, you will discover practical strategies, heartfelt stories, and insightful reflections that will guide you in building unwavering confidence.

Each chapter invites you to explore your strengths, confront your fears, and embrace the unique journey that is yours alone. Remember, confidence is not an innate trait reserved for a select few; it is a skill that can be cultivated through practice, perseverance, and self-compassion.

As you turn these pages, may you find encouragement, motivation, and the tools you need to step boldly into your future. The time to invest in yourself is now, and the possibilities are limitless.

Welcome to the journey of self-discovery and empowerment.

Preface

Confidence is a vital ingredient in the recipe for personal success and fulfillment. Yet, it often feels elusive, especially in a world that constantly tests our self-worth. Over the years, I have come to understand that building confidence is not a destination but a lifelong journey—one filled with both challenges and triumphs.

This book is a culmination of my experiences, insights, and the lessons I have learned along the way. It is designed for anyone who has ever felt uncertain, underestimated, or held back by their own doubts. Within these pages, you will find a blend of practical advice, relatable anecdotes, and exercises that encourage self-reflection and growth.

The aim of this book is not only to empower you to become more confident but also to foster a deeper understanding of yourself. By embracing your unique strengths and confronting your fears, you can unlock the door to personal development and create a life that resonates with your true self.

As you read, I encourage you to approach each chapter with an open mind and heart. Take the time to reflect on your own experiences and consider how the concepts presented can be applied to your life. Remember, every small step you take toward building your confidence contributes to the larger journey of self-discovery and empowerment.

Thank you for joining me on this adventure. May you find inspiration and courage within these pages as you embark on your own path to confidence.

Acknowledgements

Writing this book has been a deeply rewarding journey, and I am grateful to everyone who has supported and inspired me along the way.

First and foremost, I want to express my deepest gratitude to my father, who, though no longer with us, remains a guiding light in my life. Even in his absence, his presence is with me every day. His wisdom, his strength, and his love live on in my heart, and I feel him with me, encouraging me at every step. Dad, your spirit has been a source of unwavering support, and I am forever grateful for everything you've given me.

To my mother, who has been my steadfast foundation—thank you for your strength and resilience. You have been my rock, holding our family together with grace and love, and showing me the power of unwavering belief and determination. Your strength is a constant reminder of what it means to be grounded and steadfast, and I owe so much to you for the values you've instilled in me.

To my wife, Maneka, the pillar of my life—you have been my partner in every sense. Your unwavering support, understanding, and love have carried me through the hardest days and brightest moments. Thank you for standing by me, for being my constant source of encouragement, and for sharing this journey with me. I couldn't have done this without you.

And to my son, Aarav, who fills my life with joy and purpose, thank you for giving me a reason to dream bigger and strive harder. Your innocence and curiosity inspire me every day.

To my family and friends, your encouragement and belief in me have been the fuel I needed to pursue this project. Each of you holds a special place in my heart. Thank you for your support, your patience, and your love. This accomplishment is as much yours as it is mine.

To my mentors and teachers, I extend my heartfelt gratitude. Thank you for the invaluable wisdom you've shared and for guiding me on my growth path. Your insights have been a beacon in my journey, helping me to understand true confidence and purpose. You've not only shaped my mind but have also inspired me to strive to make a difference in the lives of others. I am profoundly grateful for your guidance and for the faith you've placed in me.

I also want to express my deep appreciation for the many individuals who have shared their personal stories with me. Your courage and openness have touched me in ways words can't fully capture. You've reminded me of the beauty of vulnerability and the strength in connection, and these pages are filled with the inspiration you've given me. Your stories are a testament to the resilience of the human spirit, and they have made this work infinitely more meaningful.

Thank you to each of you for your trust, your courage, and for showing me what it means to be truly connected in this shared journey. This book is as much yours as it is mine.

A special thank you to my editor and the entire publishing team, whose expertise and dedication brought this book to life. Your belief in this project has been invaluable.

Finally, I extend my heartfelt appreciation to you, the reader. Thank you for embarking on this journey with me. I hope you find the tools and inspiration you need to cultivate your own confidence and embrace your true potential.

Together, let's continue to grow, learn, and uplift one another.

Prologue

In a world where external pressures often dictate our self-worth, the quest for confidence can feel daunting. Many of us grapple with self-doubt, comparing ourselves to others and questioning our abilities. Yet, the ability to cultivate genuine confidence is not only possible; it is transformative.

This book is born from a simple but profound belief: that everyone has the capacity to grow, to believe in themselves, and to create a life that aligns with their true potential. Its purpose is to guide you through the intricacies of building confidence, providing you with practical tools, reflective exercises, and insightful stories that illuminate the journey of personal development.

Throughout these pages, you will explore a range of topics—from understanding the roots of your self-doubt to embracing vulnerability as a strength. Each chapter is designed to empower you, encouraging you to confront your fears and celebrate your unique journey. This book is not just a collection of theories; it's a roadmap that invites you to take actionable steps toward self-discovery and empowerment.

The significance of this work lies in its ability to spark change—not just within individuals, but also in communities. When we cultivate confidence in ourselves, we create a ripple effect, inspiring those around us to embrace their own journeys. This book aims to foster a culture of support, resilience, and growth, reminding us that we are not alone in our struggles.

As you delve into the content, remember that the path to confidence is a personal one. Embrace the process, allow yourself to learn and evolve, and know that every step you take brings you closer to the authentic self you were meant to be.

Welcome to a journey of self-exploration, empowerment, and confidence. Let's embark on this adventure together.

The Confidence Code

CHAPTER ONE

Cracking the Confidence Code

Confidence isn't just an abstract concept; it's a blend of mindset, behavior, and emotions. Understanding the science behind confidence can empower you to cultivate it. Learn how your thoughts, actions, and feelings interplay to shape your self-perception and outward confidence.

Understanding Confidence:

Confidence is not just a state of mind; it's a skill that can be developed and strengthened over time. Whether you're preparing for a presentation, a job interview, or simply navigating daily interactions, having confidence is key to achieving your goals and overcoming challenges. Here, we'll explore practical exercises and strategies to boost your confidence effectively.

Exercises to Boost Your Confidence

1)Visualization Techniques:
Exercise:
Find a quiet space where you can relax without distractions. Close your eyes and visualize yourself succeeding in a challenging situation. Picture every detail:

your posture, facial expressions, and the positive reactions of others. Engage all your senses to make the visualization vivid and real.

Benefits: Visualization helps to create a mental blueprint of success, reducing anxiety and reinforcing a positive self-image.

2)Power Poses:

Exercise:

Stand in a high-power pose for two minutes before a stressful event. This could be the classic "Batman" pose (hands on hips, feet apart) or any stance that makes you feel strong and confident. Focus on your breathing and maintain good posture.

Benefits: Power poses can increase testosterone levels and decrease cortisol (stress hormone), leading to a greater sense of confidence and reduced anxiety.

3)Positive Affirmations:

Exercise:

Create a list of affirmations that resonate with you personally. Examples include: "I am capable and competent," "I deserve success," or "I am confident in my abilities." Repeat these affirmations daily, especially in moments of self-doubt.

Benefits: Positive affirmations reprogram your subconscious mind, replacing negative self-talk with empowering beliefs.

4)Progressive Desensitization:

Exercise:

Gradually expose yourself to situations that challenge your confidence in manageable steps. Start with less intimidating scenarios and gradually increase the difficulty as you build resilience.

Benefits: This systematic approach desensitizes you to fear and builds confidence through repeated successful experiences.

5)Celebrate Your Achievements:

Exercise:

Keep a journal or a list of your accomplishments, no matter how small they may seem. Reflect on these achievements regularly to remind yourself of your capabilities and strengths.

Benefits: Celebrating successes reinforces positive behavior patterns and boosts self-esteem.

Confidence is not about being flawless; it's about trusting yourself and your abilities despite imperfections. By practicing these exercises consistently, you'll gradually enhance your self-assurance and face challenges with a renewed sense of confidence. Remember, confidence is a journey of growth and self-discovery—embrace it fully and enjoy the rewards it brings to your personal and professional life. To conclude here, Whatever you do, aim to become as good as you can. The better you are at doing something the more confident you become.

The Confidence Code

"Taming the Inner Critic (Negative self-talk can be a major barrier to confidence).

Understanding the Inner Critic:

Negative self-talk can undermine confidence, creating barriers to personal and professional growth. The inner critic often magnifies perceived flaws and mistakes, leading to self-doubt and hesitation. This chapter explores effective techniques to tame the inner critic and foster a supportive internal dialogue.

Techniques to Silence Your Inner Critic
1)Awareness Through Mindfulness:
Exercise: Practice mindfulness by observing your thoughts without judgment. When negative self-talk arises, acknowledge it without attaching meaning or validity to those thoughts. Focus on your breath to stay grounded in the present moment.

Benefits: Mindfulness cultivates awareness of negative thought patterns, enabling you to detach from them and choose more constructive responses.

2)Challenge Negative Thoughts:
Exercise: Write down your negative thoughts as they occur. Then, challenge each thought by asking yourself: "Is this thought based on facts or assumptions?" "Would I say this to a friend in the same situation?"
Benefits: This exercise helps to identify irrational beliefs and replace them with more balanced and realistic perspectives.

3)Practice Self-Compassion:
Exercise: Treat yourself with the same kindness and understanding you would offer to a friend facing a challenge. Write a compassionate letter to yourself, acknowledging your strengths and embracing your imperfections as part of being human.
Benefits: Self-compassion fosters resilience and reduces the impact of self-criticism, allowing you to bounce back from setbacks with greater ease.

4)Reframe Negative Statements:
Exercise: Transform negative statements into affirmations of self-worth and capability. For example, replace "I'm not good enough" with "I am learning and growing every day." Repeat these positive reframes daily to reinforce a supportive internal dialogue.
Benefits: Reframing shifts your focus from limitations to possibilities, empowering you to approach challenges with confidence.

5)Limit Comparison and Perfectionism:
Exercise: Recognize when you're comparing yourself unfavorably to others or setting unrealistic standards of perfection. Shift your focus to personal progress and improvement rather than external validation.
Benefits: Letting go of perfectionism and comparison frees you to embrace your unique journey and achievements.

Conclusion
Taming the inner critic is essential for cultivating lasting confidence and self-esteem. By practicing these techniques consistently, you'll gradually transform negative self-talk into positive self-affirmation. Embrace self-compassion as a cornerstone of your growth journey, and remember that nurturing a supportive internal dialogue is a powerful tool for building resilience and achieving your goals.

Taming the inner critic

Reframing Your Reality. (Life is full of challenges, but how you perceive them makes all the difference).

Reframing Your Reality

Life presents us with myriad challenges, each offering a chance to either stumble or grow. Central to navigating these challenges is the art of reframing—shifting our perspectives to see opportunities where others see obstacles. Reframing allows us to transform negative experiences into valuable lessons, cultivating resilience and bolstering our confidence in the process.

Exercises:

Identifying Limiting Beliefs:
Take a moment to reflect on a recent setback or challenge you faced.
Write down any negative thoughts or beliefs that arose from this experience.
Now, challenge these beliefs by asking yourself: "What can I learn from this situation?" or "How can I grow stronger from this experience?"
Reframe these negative beliefs into positive affirmations or statements that empower you.

Seeking Alternative Perspectives:
Think of a current issue or challenge in your life.
Write down how you currently perceive this issue and the emotions it evokes.
Next, imagine you are a friend or mentor looking at the same issue. How might they perceive it differently?
List at least three alternative perspectives that could exist for this situation.
Reflect on how adopting one of these alternative perspectives could change your approach to the challenge.

Turning Setbacks into Stepping Stones:
Recall a significant setback or failure from your past.
Write a brief narrative describing the event and how it initially impacted you.
Now, reflect on what you learned from that experience and how it contributed to your personal growth.
Consider how you might reframe that setback today as a pivotal moment that led to positive change or new opportunities.
Write down three lessons you can carry forward from that

experience to help you navigate future challenges with greater confidence.

Daily Reframing Practice:
Choose a specific time each day (morning or evening) to practice reframing.
Reflect on one challenging situation or negative thought you encountered during the day.
Write down three positive aspects or potential opportunities that could arise from this situation.
Challenge yourself to see beyond the immediate difficulty and explore how this experience might contribute to your personal growth journey.

Gratitude and Reframing:
Practice gratitude by listing three things you are grateful for each day.
Choose one item from your gratitude list and reflect on how it has positively impacted your life.
Explore how reframing could enhance your appreciation for this aspect of your life even further.
Write down one way you can actively incorporate this mindset of gratitude and reframing into your daily routine to strengthen your overall sense of confidence and resilience.

These exercises are designed to help you develop the skill of reframing, empowering you to turn challenges into opportunities for growth and fostering a deeper sense of confidence in your ability to navigate life's ups and downs.

Reframing the Reality

Building Confidence in a Connected World

CHAPTER FOUR

Beyond the Likes

Social media can be a double-edged sword when it comes to confidence. This chapter offers strategies to navigate the complexities of social media, fostering a positive online presence that boosts rather than diminishes your confidence.

In today's digital age, social media plays a significant role in shaping our perceptions of ourselves and others. While it can be a powerful tool for connection and self-expression, it also presents challenges to our confidence and self-esteem. This chapter explores strategies to navigate the complexities of social media, empowering you to cultivate a positive online presence that enhances rather than undermines your confidence.

1)Understanding the Impact of Social Media
Social media platforms often highlight curated versions of people's lives, showcasing achievements, milestones, and seemingly perfect moments. This curated reality can create a distorted comparison trap, where individuals measure their worth against unrealistic standards. Understanding this dynamic is crucial to reclaiming control over how you engage with social media and how it affects your

confidence. Dr Pratima Murthy ,a leading mental health expert states that Social media validation harms your Self-Esteem and Mental Well-being (Check-out on Youtube the interview conducted by The Better India)

2)Strategies for Confidence-Boosting Social Media Use
Mindful Consumption:
Take inventory of the social media accounts you follow.
Identify accounts that inspire and uplift you versus those that evoke negative feelings or comparisons.
Unfollow or mute accounts that consistently make you feel inadequate or anxious.
Curate your feed to include content that aligns with your values and aspirations, fostering a more positive digital environment.

3)Authentic Self-Presentation:
Reflect on how you present yourself on social media.
Aim for authenticity by sharing genuine moments and reflections rather than only highlighting achievements or perfect images.
Embrace vulnerability by sharing challenges and lessons learned, fostering deeper connections with your audience.
Consider how aligning your online persona with your true self can cultivate a sense of authenticity and confidence both online and offline.

4)Setting Boundaries:
Establish boundaries around your social media use to protect your mental and emotional well-being.
Designate specific times during the day for checking social media and avoid mindless scrolling.
Create tech-free zones or periods, such as during meals

or before bedtime, to promote offline connection and relaxation.Practice saying no to comparison and embrace the uniqueness of your own journey and achievements.

Exercises:

Social Media Reflection:

Spend 15-20 minutes reflecting on your recent experiences with social media.

Write down any emotions or thoughts that arise when you engage with different platforms.

Identify one positive aspect and one challenge you've encountered related to your social media use.

Brainstorm one action you can take to enhance the positive impact of social media on your confidence and well-being.

Curating Your Digital Space:

Review your current list of followers and accounts you follow across your social media platforms.

Identify at least three accounts that consistently inspire or uplift you.

Consider unfollowing or muting accounts that promote unrealistic expectations or negative emotions.

Reflect on how curating your digital space can contribute to a more positive online experience and enhance your confidence.

Authenticity Check-In:

Take a moment to review your recent social media posts.

Evaluate whether your posts reflect your authentic self or if they primarily portray a curated image.

Identify one aspect of your life or personality that you could share more authentically with your audience.

Write a draft of a post that showcases this authenticity,

aiming to inspire genuine connection and confidence in your online presence.

Benefits of Positive Social Media Engagement:

Enhanced Self-Acceptance:
By curating a positive digital environment, you reinforce self-acceptance and celebrate your unique journey. Authentic self-expression on social media fosters confidence by encouraging genuine connections and reducing the pressure to conform to unrealistic standards. Setting boundaries and mindful consumption habits empower you to use social media as a tool for growth and connection rather than comparison and insecurity.

By implementing these strategies and exercises, you can harness the potential of social media to boost your confidence, cultivate authenticity, and foster meaningful connections in both your digital and offline life.

Life > Likes

CHAPTER FIVE

Perfectionism can be Paralyzing

Perfectionism can be paralyzing. Embrace vulnerability as a source of strength and connection. Learn how opening up about your imperfections can enhance your relationships and build authentic confidence.

Embracing vulnerability as a source of strength and connection can indeed be transformative.Vulnerability generally refers to the state of being exposed to the possibility of being harmed, either physically or emotionally. In emotional contexts, vulnerability often involves opening oneself up to others, revealing one's true feelings, weaknesses, or uncertainties, which can lead to a deeper connection but also entails the risk of rejection or hurt. It's a fundamental aspect of human relationships and personal growth, often associated with authenticity and courage. Here's how it benefits individuals and some exercises towards achieving it:

Benefits of Embracing Vulnerability:
Authenticity and Connection: When you allow yourself to be vulnerable, you show your true self to others. This authenticity deepens connections as people can relate to

your struggles and imperfections.

Emotional Resilience: Facing vulnerability builds emotional resilience. It teaches you that it's okay to make mistakes or to not have all the answers, which reduces fear and anxiety about being judged.

Enhanced Relationships: Vulnerability fosters empathy and trust in relationships. It encourages open communication and allows others to reciprocate by sharing their vulnerabilities, thereby strengthening the bond.

Personal Growth: Being vulnerable means confronting your fears and insecurities. This process of self-reflection and acceptance promotes personal growth and self-awareness.

Reflect on Your Imperfections: Be yourself and make a list of your perceived imperfections or weaknesses,
This exercise helps you acknowledge areas where they might feel vulnerable.

Seek Feedback and Accept Criticism: Seek constructive feedback from trusted individuals. And accept criticism gracefully as a tool for growth rather than viewing it as a personal attack. This is the attitude, the one who cant work on himself no one other can ever help him out. Your life is your responsibility not anyone's business

Challenge Perfectionistic Tendencies: Break down larger goals into smaller, manageable tasks. For instance, if someone wants to write a book, suggest they start by writing for 30 minutes a day rather than aiming to finish a whole chapter in one sitting.

The purpose of this exercise help shift focus from achieving perfection (e.g., writing a flawless chapter) to making steady progress (e.g., writing consistently). It teaches that progress is more important than perfection and allows for learning and adjustment along the way.
I am addressing it to encourage you to set realistic goals and embrace mistakes as opportunities for learning.

Seeking Help or Guidance:

Example: In the year 2023 I was looking to buy my first own house in Mumbai, because I didn't had any money to go for and the my known people for suggested to drop the plan for this time and wait for some time for the next opportunity and it was happened with all the blessings and guidance, irrespective without or very less cooperation from the seller and he misguided and scammed, by the grace of god everything happened peacefully,during that tough time one iron lady was beside me and time and again she always guided and directed from my childhood day Ms Vatsala , I am always grateful and blessed to have pillar like her beside me and "I'm thankful for having the courage to ask for help from her. Despite feeling vulnerable,guidance from her has been invaluable. And the support has helped me navigate from this situation, and I'm grateful for her kindness and understanding."

Conclusion:

By incorporating these exercises, story and understanding the benefits of embracing vulnerability,I want to cultivate authentic confidence in you. And learn that vulnerability isn't a weakness but a powerful tool for personal and relational growth. This approach encourages you to step out of their comfort zones, connect more deeply with others, and ultimately enhance their overall well-being.

Don't wait for Perfection

CHAPTER SIX

The Global Stage

In today's interconnected and fast-paced business world, effective communication stands as a pivotal skills for mid and senior-level executives aiming to navigate diverse cultural landscapes and command influence in any setting. This chapter is crafted to provide comprehensive strategies that not only alleviate anxieties associated with public speaking but also enhance cross-cultural communication proficiency, enabling executives to exude confidence and assertiveness on the global stage.

Benefits of Effective Communication:

Communication works for those who work at it." — John Powell.

Mastering communication enables executives to articulate their vision clearly, inspiring teams and stakeholders alike.

Stronger Relationships: To effectively communicate, we must realize that we are all different in the way we perceive the world and use this understanding as a guide to our communication with others." — Tony Robbins. Cultivating cross-cultural communication skills fosters trust and empathy, essential for building lasting global relationships.

Improved Leadership Presence: The way we communicate with others and with ourselves ultimately determines the quality of our lives." — Tony Robbins. Confident communication establishes credibility and authority, crucial for effective leadership in diverse and challenging environments.

Exercises to Enhance Communication Skills:

1.Visualization and Mental Rehearsal:

Envision successful speaking engagements to boost confidence and reduce anxiety.Practicing in front of a mirror or with trusted peers can refine delivery and presence.

2.Cross-Cultural Role-Playing:

Cross-Cultural role playing enables us to immerse ourselves in diverse perspective, fostering empathy and deepening our understanding of global interconnectedness.Engage in role-playing exercises to simulate cross-cultural interactions, emphasizing adaptability and cultural sensitivity.

3.Feedback and Improvement:

Communication – the human connection – is the key to personal and career success." — Paul J. Meyer. Seek feedback from mentors, colleagues, or professional coaches to continuously refine communication effectiveness and message clarity.

Strategies for Effective Communication:

Preparation and Structure:By failing to prepare, you are preparing to fail. — Benjamin Franklin. Develop a systematic approach to preparing presentations, including thorough research, clear messaging, and anticipating audience reactions.

Cultural Sensitivity Training:Invest in ongoing learning about cultural norms and communication preferences of international counterparts. The single biggest problem in communication is the illusion that it has taken place." —

George Bernard Shaw.

Body Language Mastery:Actions speak louder than words." — Abraham Lincoln. Master non-verbal communication cues such as posture, gestures, and eye contact to enhance presence and convey confidence.

Lead by Example:Demonstrate effective communication in your own interactions to set a standard for your team.

Create Opportunities:Foster an environment where team members can practice and improve their communication skills through workshops, mentoring, and real-world scenarios.

Feedback and Development:Provide constructive feedback and opportunities for growth to empower team members to become confident communicators.

By integrating these strategies and exercises into their professional development, executives can elevate their communication prowess, bridge cultural divides with finesse, and ultimately establish a compelling presence on the global stage.

BHAVESH POOJARI

Be at Global Stage

• 29 •

CHAPTER SEVEN

Building Bridges, Not Walls (Fostering Empathy and Strong Relationships)

In today's interconnected world, empathy and strong relationships are foundational not only to personal happiness but also to professional success.

This chapter explores the critical role of empathy in cultivating meaningful connections that enhance confidence and support individual goals.

Fostering Empathy and Strong Relationships:

Enhanced Emotional Intelligence:

Developing empathy allows individuals to understand and resonate with the emotions of others, thereby strengthening emotional intelligence and interpersonal dynamics.

Strengthened Collaboration:

Building strong relationships fosters teamwork and collaboration. It enables individuals to work effectively with diverse teams, leveraging collective strengths to achieve shared objectives.

Increased Resilience:

Genuine relationships provide a support system during challenges and setbacks. They contribute to mental well-being and resilience, offering emotional sustenance and encouragement.

Exercises

Active Listening Practices:Engage in active listening by focusing intently on what others are saying without distractions or interruptions. Reflect on their feelings and perspectives to deepen mutual understanding.

Perspective-Taking Exercises:Practice seeing situations from different viewpoints. This exercise fosters empathy by encouraging individuals to consider diverse perspectives and appreciate varying experiences.

Building Rapport:Cultivate trust and rapport through genuine interactions. Show empathy by demonstrating genuine interest, respect, and support for others' well-being and success.

Actionable

Practice Gratitude:Express appreciation for others' contributions and qualities regularly. Recognize and acknowledge their efforts to create a positive and supportive environment.

Conflict Resolution Skills:Develop skills to resolve conflicts constructively. Focus on listening actively, seeking common ground, and working toward mutually beneficial solutions.

Networking with Purpose:Build professional relationships intentionally. Seek to understand others' goals and aspirations, and offer support and assistance where possible.

By incorporating these exercises and actionable strategies into daily interactions, individuals can cultivate empathy, strengthen relationships, and enhance their confidence both personally and professionally. This chapter aims to empower readers to build bridges of understanding and connection, fostering a collaborative environment where everyone can thrive and succeed.

Building bridges not Walls

Cultivating Confidence Through Action

Fake it Till You Make It (the Right Way) The Science of Confidence-Building Behaviors

Confidence is a dynamic skill that can be nurtured through deliberate actions and behaviors. This chapter explores the concept of "fake it till you make it" in a constructive manner, revealing how adopting confident behaviors can profoundly enhance self-perception and cultivate genuine confidence.

Understanding Confidence-Building Behaviors:
Confidence is often seen as a byproduct of external validation or past successes. However, behavioral psychology suggests that confidence can also be cultivated through intentional actions and positive behaviors. By consciously engaging in behaviors associated with

confidence, individuals can reshape their internal beliefs and enhance their self-image.

The Power of Acting "As If":
Acting "as if" involves embodying behaviors that reflect confidence, even in situations where self-doubt may arise. This approach leverages the principle of behavioral activation, where actions can precede emotions. Over time, consistently practicing confident behaviors rewires the brain, reinforcing a more resilient and self-assured mindset.

Benefits of Adopting Confident Behaviors:
Enhanced Self-Perception: Practicing confident behaviors boosts self-esteem and fosters a positive self-image, leading to greater self-assurance in personal and professional endeavors.

Increased Resilience: Confidence-building behaviors equip individuals with the resilience to navigate challenges effectively, bouncing back stronger from setbacks.

Improved Relationships: Confidence enhances interpersonal relationships by promoting assertiveness, effective communication, and mutual respect.

Career Advancement: Confidence is attractive to employers and colleagues alike, opening doors to leadership roles, promotions, and new opportunities.

Reduced Stress: Adopting confident behaviors reduces anxiety and stress levels, enabling individuals to approach tasks and challenges with a calm and composed demeanor.

Exercises to Develop Authentic Confidence:

Visualization Techniques: Visualize yourself succeeding in challenging situations. Imagine the feelings of confidence and accomplishment associated with achieving your goals.

Role-Playing Scenarios: Practice assertive communication and confident body language through role-playing exercises. Simulate scenarios where you confidently express your ideas or negotiate effectively.

Power Pose Ritual: Incorporate power poses into your daily routine. Stand tall with hands on hips or arms raised for a few minutes each day to boost feelings of confidence and empowerment.

Challenge Limiting Beliefs: Identify and challenge negative or limiting beliefs about your abilities. Replace these beliefs with affirmations that reinforce your strengths and capabilities.

Step Out of Comfort Zones: Gradually expand your comfort zones by volunteering for public speaking opportunities, taking on leadership responsibilities, or networking with new contacts.

Actionable Strategies for Adopting Confident Behaviors:

Set Clear Goals: Define specific goals that align with your vision of confidence and break them down into manageable steps.

Practice Gratitude: Cultivate a mindset of gratitude by acknowledging your achievements and strengths daily.

Seek Feedback: Solicit constructive feedback from mentors or trusted peers to gain insights into areas where you can further develop confidence.

Continuous Learning: Invest in personal and professional development to acquire new skills and knowledge that contribute to your confidence.

Celebrate Progress: Celebrate milestones and successes along your journey to building authentic confidence, reinforcing positive behaviors and habits.

By integrating these exercises and actionable strategies into your daily routine, you can cultivate authentic confidence and enhance your overall well-being. This chapter aims to empower readers to embrace the transformative potential of behavior in shaping their beliefs and achieving sustained confidence and success.

Fake it till you make it

The Power of Small Wins The practical strategies for setting and achieving incremental goals.

Big goals can be overwhelming, but breaking them down into smaller, achievable steps can boost motivation and sustain confidence.

In the pursuit of confidence and success, tackling big goals can often feel daunting and overwhelming.

However, breaking these larger objectives into smaller, manageable steps not only makes them more achievable but also enhances motivation and sustains confidence.

This chapter explores the transformative impact of setting and achieving incremental goals.

Benefits of Setting Incremental Goals:

1.Enhanced Motivation:

Small wins provide immediate feedback and a sense of accomplishment, fueling motivation to pursue larger objectives.

2. Builds Momentum:

Achieving smaller goals creates positive momentum, making it easier to stay focused and committed to long-term aspirations.

3.Boosts Confidence:

Each small success reinforces belief in one's abilities, building self-assurance and resilience in the face of challenges.

4.Promotes Learning and Growth:

Incremental goals encourage continuous learning and skill development, fostering personal and professional growth.

5. Reduces Procrastination:

Breaking tasks into smaller steps minimizes overwhelm and procrastination, making progress more manageable and sustainable.

Exercises to Set and Achieve Incremental Goals:**

1. SMART Goal Setting:

Define goals that are Specific, Measurable, Achievable, Relevant, and Time-bound. Break down larger goals into smaller milestones.

2. Prioritization Techniques:

Use techniques such as Eisenhower Matrix or ABC prioritization to identify and focus on the most critical tasks.

3. Progress Tracking:
Create a visual tracker or journal to monitor progress toward your goals. Celebrate each milestone achieved along the way.

4. Daily Habits and Routines:
Establish daily habits that support your goals, such as setting aside dedicated time for focused work or skill development.

5. Accountability Partnerships:
Partner with a friend, mentor, or coach who can provide support, accountability, and feedback on your progress.

Actionable Strategies for Achieving Incremental Goals:

1. Break Down Goals:
Divide larger goals into smaller, actionable steps that you can tackle one at a time.

2. Celebrate Small Wins:
Acknowledge and celebrate each achievement, no matter how small, to reinforce positive behavior and maintain motivation.

3. Adjust and Adapt:
Be flexible in adjusting your approach based on feedback and changing circumstances, while staying focused on the end goal.

4. Review and Reflect:
Regularly review your progress and reflect on lessons learned. Adjust your goals and strategies as needed to stay on track.

5. Continuous Improvement: Strive for continuous improvement by seeking feedback, learning from setbacks, and refining your skills and approaches.

By implementing these strategies and exercises, individuals can harness the power of small wins to build momentum, sustain motivation, and achieve long-term success with confidence. This chapter aims to empower readers to embrace incremental progress as a pathway to realizing their full potential and enhancing their overall confidence in every aspect of life.

Small Win Matters

CHAPTER TEN

Stepping Out of Your Comfort Zone

Taking risks is essential for growth. Discuss the importance of stepping out of your comfort zone and embracing failure as a learning opportunity. Learn how calculated risks can lead to significant confidence gains.

Confidence is not just about feeling secure in familiar situations; it's also about embracing challenges and uncertainty to foster personal growth.

This chapter explores the importance of stepping out of your comfort zone, embracing failure as a learning opportunity, and how calculated risks can lead to significant gains in confidence.

Benefits of Stepping Out of Your Comfort Zone:

1. Personal Growth:

Embracing challenges promotes personal development and resilience, expanding your skills and capabilities.

2. Expanded Comfort Zone:

Each new experience outside your comfort zone enlarges your comfort zone, making future challenges seem more manageable.

3. Increased Self-Efficacy:
Overcoming obstacles boosts self-belief and confidence in your ability to handle unfamiliar situations.

4.Enhanced Adaptability:
Stepping out of your comfort zone improves adaptability and flexibility in navigating change and uncertainty.

5. Opportunity for Innovation:
Trying new things fosters creativity and innovation, leading to fresh perspectives and breakthrough solutions.

Exercises to Step Out of Your Comfort Zone:

1.Identify Fear-Based Limits:
Identify specific fears or discomforts that hold you back from taking risks or trying new experiences.

2. Gradual Exposure:
Start with small steps outside your comfort zone, gradually increasing the level of challenge as you build confidence.

3. Mindfulness and Relaxation Techniques:
Use mindfulness or relaxation exercises to manage anxiety and maintain focus when facing challenges.

4. Seek Feedback:
Request feedback from mentors or peers to gain insights and perspectives on your performance and areas for

improvement.

5. Reflective Journaling:
Keep a journal to track your experiences, thoughts, and emotions as you step outside your comfort zone. Reflect on lessons learned and growth achieved.

Actionable Strategies for Embracing Risks:

1. Set Clear Goals:
Define specific goals that require you to step out of your comfort zone. Break them down into actionable steps.

2. Challenge Negative Thoughts:
Replace self-limiting beliefs with affirmations and positive self-talk that reinforce your capability to handle challenges.

3. Visualize Success:
Visualize yourself successfully navigating challenging situations. Imagine the feelings of confidence and accomplishment associated with overcoming obstacles.

4. Build a Support Network:
Surround yourself with supportive individuals who encourage and motivate you to take risks and grow.

5.Celebrate Progress
Acknowledge and celebrate each step taken outside your comfort zone, regardless of the outcome, to reinforce courage and resilience.

By embracing risks and stepping out of your comfort zone, individuals can cultivate resilience, expand their capabilities, and enhance their overall confidence.

This chapter aims to empower readers to embrace discomfort as a pathway to personal growth and achievement, ultimately strengthening their belief in their ability to thrive in any situation.

Comfort Zone < Magic Zone

CHAPTER ELEVEN

Body Language for Success || Charlie Chaplin || Mr.Bean || Aura of Mr Amitabh

Nonverbal communication plays a crucial role in projecting confidence. This chapter equips you with body language techniques to help you convey power and confidence in any situation.

Nonverbal communication is a powerful tool in projecting confidence. While words can articulate our thoughts, body language conveys our feelings and attitudes in a more immediate and impactful manner. In this chapter, we'll explore how to harness body language to exude confidence, drawing inspiration from iconic figures like Charlie Chaplin and Mr. Bean, and examining the aura of Amitabh Bachchan. We'll also discuss practical exercises to refine your nonverbal communication skills.

The Power of Nonverbal Communication

Nonverbal communication encompasses facial expressions, gestures, posture, and eye contact. These elements can either reinforce or undermine your spoken words. For example, a confident posture and steady eye contact can enhance your authority and approachability, while closed body language or lack of eye contact may suggest insecurity or disinterest.

Lessons from Iconic Figures

Charlie Chaplin: Mastering the Art of Expressive Movement
Charlie Chaplin, the legendary silent film star, is a prime example of how body language can transcend words. His expressive gestures and nuanced movements conveyed complex emotions and stories, engaging audiences without a single spoken line. Chaplin's ability to communicate confidence and charm through his physical presence teaches us the importance of clarity and intention in our movements.

By adopting Chaplin's techniques, you can learn to express yourself more vividly and ensure that your body language aligns with your message, enhancing overall impact.

Practice conveying a simple emotion (like happiness or frustration) using only your body.
Record yourself and review how effectively you communicate the emotion without words.

Mr. Bean: Confidence Through Quirkiness**
Mr. Bean, portrayed by Rowan Atkinson, is known for his unique and often comical body language. Despite his non-verbal approach, Mr. Bean exudes confidence through his exaggerated and purposeful movements. His character's ability to navigate various situations with a distinctive style demonstrates how confidence can be expressed through individuality and a strong sense of self.

Emulating Mr. Bean's approach can help you embrace your personal quirks and use them to project confidence. Understanding that confidence doesn't always mean conforming can be empowering.
Identify your own unique mannerisms or quirks. Practice incorporating them into your interactions, ensuring they convey positive and confident traits.

Amitabh Bachchan: The Aura of Commanding Presence
Amitabh Bachchan, the iconic Bollywood actor, commands respect and authority through his body language. His posture, steady gaze, and deliberate movements contribute to his powerful presence. Bachchan's aura is a testament to the impact of maintaining strong, confident body language.

Adopting a commanding posture and deliberate movements can enhance your presence and make you appear more authoritative and self-assured.
Practice standing and sitting with a strong posture. Focus on maintaining a straight back, relaxed shoulders, and steady eye contact in various scenarios. Pay attention to

how these changes influence others' perceptions of you.

Practical Techniques for Projecting Confidence

1. Posture: Stand and sit up straight with your shoulders back. A strong, open posture improves how others perceive you and boosts your self-esteem.

2. Eye Contact: Maintain steady eye contact during conversations. It demonstrates confidence and interest, helping to build trust and rapport.

3. Gestures: Use purposeful gestures to emphasize points and convey enthusiasm. Avoid fidgeting or crossing your arms, as these can signal discomfort or defensiveness.

4. Facial Expressions:
Ensure your facial expressions align with your message. A genuine smile can make you appear more approachable and confident.

5.Voice Modulation: While not purely body language, your voice plays a crucial role in conveying confidence. Practice speaking clearly and with varied intonation to keep your audience engaged and assertive.

Exercises and Practices

1. Mirror Practice:
Stand in front of a mirror and practice different facial expressions and gestures. Observe how your body language

affects your appearance and adjust accordingly.

2. Role-Playing:
Engage in role-playing exercises where you adopt different body language styles. Experiment with confident and less confident postures to see how they influence your interactions.

3. Feedback Sessions:
Ask friends or colleagues for feedback on your body language. Use their observations to make adjustments and enhance your nonverbal communication skills.

4. Mindfulness and Awareness:
Incorporate mindfulness techniques to become more aware of your body language in real-time. Practice observing and adjusting your posture, gestures, and expressions throughout the day.

Conclusion

Mastering body language is a crucial step towards projecting confidence and achieving success. By learning from the expressive movement of Charlie Chaplin, the unique quirkiness of Mr. Bean, and the commanding presence of Amitabh Bachchan, you can refine your nonverbal communication skills. Incorporate these techniques and exercises into your daily routine to enhance your confidence and leave a lasting impression in every interaction.

Body Language for Success

Confidence – A Lifelong Journey

CHAPTER TWELVE

The Imposter Syndrome (Unveiling the Truth)

Imposter Syndrome is a psychological phenomenon where individuals doubt their accomplishments and constantly fear being exposed as a "fraud." This experience is prevalent among high achievers and can significantly undermine self-confidence. Despite evidence of their competence, those affected often feel they do not deserve their success and worry that others will eventually discover their perceived inadequacies. In this chapter, we will delve into the nature of Imposter Syndrome, explore its impact, and offer practical strategies to overcome it and build lasting confidence.

Understanding Imposter Syndrome
Imposter Syndrome can affect anyone, but it is especially common among high achievers. People experiencing this syndrome may believe their success is due to luck rather than skill or talent. They might also attribute their achievements to the support of others rather than their

efforts. Common thoughts associated with Imposter Syndrome include:

"I only succeeded because I was in the right place at the right time."
"People will find out that I'm not as capable as they think I am."
"My success is just a fluke, and I won't be able to replicate it."
These thoughts can lead to chronic stress, anxiety, and a lack of confidence. Individuals may continuously strive to prove themselves while fearing that their true inadequacies will be exposed. This internal conflict can create a cycle of self-doubt and hinder personal and professional growth.

The Impact of Imposter Syndrome
Imposter Syndrome can have several negative effects on both personal well-being and professional performance:

Chronic Stress and Anxiety: The constant fear of being exposed as a fraud can lead to high levels of stress and anxiety. This mental strain can affect overall health and well-being.

Burnout: The relentless drive to prove oneself and the pressure to maintain a façade of competence can lead to burnout. This exhaustion can diminish motivation and productivity.

Reduced Self-Esteem: Imposter Syndrome can erode self-esteem by reinforcing feelings of inadequacy and self-doubt. This diminished self-worth can affect various aspects of life, including relationships and career advancement.

Stagnation in Personal and Professional Growth: The fear of failure and exposure may prevent individuals from taking on new challenges or pursuing opportunities that could lead to growth and advancement.

Benefits of Overcoming Imposter Syndrome
Addressing and overcoming Imposter Syndrome can lead to significant improvements in various areas of life:

Enhanced Self-Esteem: By recognizing and addressing imposter feelings, you can validate your achievements and acknowledge your true capabilities, leading to healthier self-esteem.

Increased Resilience: Overcoming these feelings helps build resilience, making it easier to handle setbacks and continue pursuing your goals without being paralyzed by fear.

Improved Performance: Confidence in your abilities allows you to focus more on performance and growth, rather than being preoccupied with self-doubt.

Better Relationships: Letting go of the need to constantly prove yourself can lead to more authentic and fulfilling interactions with others, both personally and professionally.

Exercises and Practices for Overcoming Imposter Syndrome
Acknowledge Your Feelings

Practice: Start by writing down specific instances where you've felt like an imposter. Reflect on these moments to identify any patterns or triggers. Acknowledge these feelings without judgment and understand that they are common among high achievers.

Benefit: This exercise helps you recognize that imposter feelings are not unique to you and are often experienced by many. Understanding this can alleviate some of the anxiety associated with these feelings.

Document Your Achievements

Practice: Create a "success journal" where you regularly record your accomplishments, positive feedback, and milestones. Include detailed descriptions of your achievements and the effort you put into them.

Benefit: Reviewing your success journal reinforces your competence by providing tangible evidence of your skills and accomplishments. This can help counteract imposter feelings and build confidence.

Reframe Your Thoughts

Practice: Whenever you catch yourself having imposter thoughts, actively challenge them by reframing the situation. For example, if you think, "I was just lucky," reframe it to, "I worked hard and was prepared for the opportunity."

Benefit: Reframing helps shift your perspective from self-doubt to recognition of your efforts and skills. This cognitive shift can reduce feelings of inadequacy and increase self-confidence.

Seek Feedback and Support

Practice: Regularly seek feedback from mentors, peers, or supervisors. Use their input to understand how your work is perceived and to gain validation.

Benefit: Constructive feedback and external validation can help dispel feelings of inadequacy and build confidence. Knowing that others recognize your abilities can reinforce your self-worth.

Set Realistic Goals

Practice: Break down your larger goals into smaller, manageable tasks. Celebrate each small achievement along the way, acknowledging your progress.

Benefit: Achieving smaller milestones provides continuous validation and reinforces your sense of accomplishment. This incremental approach helps maintain motivation and reduces the impact of imposter feelings.

Visualize Success

Practice: Spend a few minutes each day visualizing yourself succeeding in your goals. Picture yourself handling challenges with confidence and competence.

Benefit: Visualization helps create a positive mindset and

reinforces your belief in your abilities. Imagining success can boost confidence and prepare you for real-life challenges.

Affirmations and Positive Self-Talk

Practice: Develop a set of positive affirmations that counteract your imposter feelings. Repeat them daily to build a more positive self-image.

Benefit: Positive self-talk can counterbalance negative thoughts and foster a more confident self-perception. Repeating affirmations helps to internalize positive beliefs about your abilities.

Engage in Professional Development

Practice: Invest in learning opportunities, such as workshops, courses, or seminars, to continually enhance your skills and knowledge.

Benefit: Gaining new skills and knowledge can boost your confidence and reduce feelings of inadequacy. Continuous learning reinforces your competence and adaptability.

Develop a Support Network

Practice: Build a support network of peers, mentors, and friends who can offer encouragement, share experiences, and provide perspective.

Benefit: Having a support network can provide emotional support and practical advice, helping you navigate challenges and reduce feelings of isolation related to imposter syndrome.

Conclusion

Imposter Syndrome is a common barrier to self-confidence, even among high achievers. By understanding its nature and implementing the strategies outlined in this chapter, you can address these feelings of self-doubt and build a more solid foundation of self-assurance. Recognizing your accomplishments, reframing negative thoughts, seeking feedback, and engaging in continuous learning are crucial steps in overcoming Imposter Syndrome. As you work through these exercises and practices, you'll find that your self-confidence grows stronger, allowing you to fully embrace your success and continue striving towards your goals with greater assurance. Embrace the truth of your achievements and capabilities, and let go of the illusion of inadequacy to unlock your full potential.

The Imposter Syndrome

CHAPTER THIRTEEN

Building Confidence in a World of Change

The world of work is constantly evolving. Equip yourself with tools to navigate change and maintain confidence in the face of uncertainty. Adaptability and resilience are key to thriving in a dynamic environment.

In today's fast-paced world, change is the only constant. The landscape of work and life is continually evolving, driven by technological advancements, shifting market dynamics, and cultural transformations. Navigating this ever-changing environment can be challenging, but you can maintain and even bolster your self-confidence with the right tools and mindset. This chapter will explore strategies for adapting to change, building resilience, and thriving in a dynamic world.

Understanding the Importance of Adaptability

Adaptability is the ability to adjust to new conditions quickly and effectively. In a world where change is ubiquitous, being adaptable allows you to remain flexible and open to new opportunities. It helps you manage stress and maintain your confidence even when faced with unexpected challenges or transitions.

Resilience, on the other hand, refers to your capacity to recover quickly from difficulties. It involves bouncing back from setbacks and continuing to pursue your goals despite obstacles. Both adaptability and resilience are crucial for thriving in an environment marked by constant change.

Benefits of Embracing Change

1.Enhanced Problem-Solving Skills:Embracing change allows you to develop and refine problem-solving skills as you learn to navigate new challenges and uncertainties.

2. Increased Innovation:Adapting to change often requires creative thinking and innovation. Embracing new ideas and approaches can lead to personal and professional growth.

3. Greater Career Opportunities:Being adaptable opens up new career opportunities by positioning you as a proactive and forward-thinking individual.

4. Improved Stress Management:Learning to handle change effectively can reduce anxiety and stress, leading to better mental and emotional well-being.

5.Strengthened Confidence:Successfully navigating change can boost your confidence, demonstrating that you are capable of handling uncertainty and adversity.

Practical Exercises and Strategies for Building Confidence Amid Change

1. Develop a Growth Mindset

A growth mindset involves viewing challenges as opportunities for learning and development. By focusing on growth rather than fixed abilities, you can approach change with a positive and proactive attitude.

Embracing a growth mindset can increase your resilience, improve your problem-solving skills, and enhance your confidence in handling new situations.

Reflect on a recent challenge or change you faced. Write down what you learned from the experience and how it contributed to your personal or professional growth. Regularly engage in self-reflection to reinforce a growth mindset.

2. Set Clear Goals and Prioritize

Setting clear goals provides direction and purpose, helping you stay focused and motivated amidst change. Prioritizing your goals ensures that you manage your time and resources effectively.

Clear goals and priorities help you maintain confidence by providing a roadmap for navigating change and achieving success.

Create a list of short-term and long-term goals. Break each goal down into actionable steps and prioritize them based on importance and urgency. Review and adjust your goals regularly to stay aligned with your evolving circumstances.

3. Build a Support Network

Surrounding yourself with a supportive network of colleagues, friends, and mentors can provide encouragement, advice, and perspective during times of change.

A strong support network can boost your confidence by offering reassurance and helping you navigate challenges more effectively.

Identify key individuals in your life who can offer support and guidance. Schedule regular check-ins with them to discuss your progress, seek feedback, and share experiences. Consider joining professional or social groups related to your interests or goals.

4.Embrace Continuous Learning

In a rapidly changing world, continuous learning is essential for staying relevant and competitive. Acquiring new skills and knowledge enhances your adaptability and confidence.

Continuous learning keeps you informed about industry trends and developments, enabling you to adapt more easily to changes and seize new opportunities.

Identify areas where you would like to expand your knowledge or skills. Enroll in courses, attend workshops, or read books and articles related to these areas. Set aside regular time for learning and self-improvement.

5.Practice Self-Care and Stress Management

Managing stress and maintaining self-care practices are crucial for maintaining confidence and resilience during times of change.

Effective stress management helps you stay calm and focused, while self-care practices support overall well-being and confidence.

Develop a self-care routine that includes activities such as exercise, meditation, healthy eating, and adequate rest. Practice stress-relief techniques, such as deep breathing, journaling, or mindfulness, to manage anxiety and maintain a balanced perspective.

6. Adapt Your Communication Skills

Effective communication is key to navigating change, both in terms of expressing your needs and understanding others' perspectives.

Strong communication skills help you build positive relationships, manage conflicts, and collaborate effectively during times of transition.

Practice active listening by giving your full attention to others during conversations. Work on articulating your thoughts clearly and assertively. Seek feedback on your communication skills and make improvements as needed.

7. Reflect on Past Successes

Reflecting on past successes and how you managed previous changes can reinforce your confidence and provide valuable insights for handling future challenges.

Revisiting your achievements and past experiences can remind you of your capabilities and strengths, boosting your confidence in navigating new situations.

Create a "success portfolio" where you document your past achievements, challenges overcome, and lessons learned. Review this portfolio regularly to remind yourself of your abilities and resilience.

8. Embrace Flexibility and Open-Mindedness

Being flexible and open-minded allows you to adapt to new ideas and approaches, making it easier to navigate change.

Flexibility and open-mindedness help you stay receptive to new opportunities and solutions, enhancing your adaptability and confidence.

Challenge yourself to try new approaches or perspectives in your daily life. Experiment with different problem-solving techniques and be open to feedback and new ideas from others.

Conclusion

Building confidence in a world of change requires a proactive approach, embracing adaptability, and developing resilience. By cultivating a growth mindset, setting clear goals, building a support network, and engaging in continuous learning, you can navigate the dynamic landscape of work and life with greater confidence. Incorporating self-care, effective communication, and reflection on past successes further strengthens your ability to handle change successfully. Embrace the opportunities that change presents, and let your confidence flourish as you adapt and thrive in an ever-evolving world.

Building Confidence

CHAPTER FOURTEEN

Lifelong Learning for Lifelong Confidence

Continuous learning and skill development are essential for maintaining and growing confidence. Embrace a mindset of lifelong learning to stay confident and competent in all areas of life.

In a world marked by rapid change and evolving dynamics, maintaining self-confidence requires more than static self-assurance.

It necessitates a proactive approach to personal and professional development through lifelong learning. Lifelong learning is not merely about accumulating knowledge but about fostering a mindset of continuous growth and adaptability. This chapter explores how embracing lifelong learning can enhance and sustain your confidence, providing practical strategies to integrate learning into your everyday life.

The Essence of Lifelong Learning

Have a student mindset

Lifelong learning is a commitment to continuously acquiring new skills and knowledge throughout your life.

This mindset is vital for several reasons:

1. Adaptability:
In an era of technological advancements and shifting market trends, being adaptable is crucial. Lifelong learning helps you stay current with new developments and adjust to changes efficiently.

2. Competence:
Regularly updating and expanding your skills ensures that you remain competent in your field. This ongoing development strengthens your confidence in your professional and personal capabilities.

3.Personal Growth:
Lifelong learning encourages personal growth by exposing you to new ideas, cultures, and experiences. This broader perspective enriches your life and keeps you engaged and curious.

4. Professional Advancement:
Continuously developing your skills and knowledge opens new career opportunities and enhances your marketability. This proactive approach reinforces your confidence in pursuing career goals and seizing new opportunities.

5. Self-Esteem:
Mastering new skills and knowledge boosts your self-esteem by demonstrating your ability to grow and adapt. This reinforces your belief in your potential and capabilities.

Benefits of Lifelong Learning for Confidence

1. Enhanced Problem-Solving Skills:
Lifelong learning exposes you to diverse problem-solving approaches and methodologies. This exposure enhances your ability to tackle complex issues and reinforces your confidence in your problem-solving skills.

2. Increased Marketability:
Acquiring new skills and knowledge makes you more competitive in the job market. This increased marketability boosts your confidence in your career prospects and professional value.

3. Broadened Perspectives:
Engaging in lifelong learning broadens your understanding of different cultures, ideas, and disciplines. This expanded perspective contributes to a more confident and well-rounded worldview.

4. Boosted Motivation:
Learning new things can reignite your passion and motivation. This renewed enthusiasm enhances your self-image and contributes to sustained confidence in your abilities.

5. Strengthened Resilience:
The process of learning and adapting to new challenges builds resilience. This resilience helps you face setbacks with greater confidence and determination.

Strategies for Embracing Lifelong Learning

1. Cultivate Curiosity

Curiosity is the driving force behind lifelong learning. Cultivating curiosity encourages you to explore new subjects, seek out new knowledge, and embrace new experiences.

A curious mindset keeps you engaged and motivated to learn, fostering continuous growth and reinforcing your confidence in acquiring new skills.

Identify topics or areas that pique your interest. Set aside regular time to explore these interests through reading, online courses, or discussions with experts. Challenge yourself to ask questions and seek answers on subjects that intrigue you.

2. Set Learning Goals

Setting clear, achievable learning goals provides direction and motivation. Goals give you a roadmap for your learning journey and a sense of accomplishment as you progress.

Specific learning goals enhance your confidence by offering a structured path for skill development and progress tracking.

Define both short-term and long-term learning goals related to your interests or career aspirations. Break each goal into actionable steps and create a timeline for achieving them. Regularly review and adjust your goals based on your progress and changing interests.

3. Seek Feedback and Reflect

Feedback from others and reflection on your learning experiences help you identify areas for improvement and celebrate your achievements.

Constructive feedback and self-reflection support continuous improvement and reinforce your confidence by highlighting your progress and areas of strength.

After completing a learning activity or project, seek feedback from peers, mentors, or supervisors. Reflect on the feedback and your experience, noting any insights or lessons learned. Use this reflection to guide future learning efforts and address areas needing improvement.

4. Leverage Technology

Technology offers a wealth of resources for learning, including online courses, webinars, podcasts, and educational apps. Leveraging these tools can enhance your learning experience and accessibility.

Utilizing technology for learning provides flexibility and convenience, making it easier to integrate learning into your busy schedule and stay current with new trends.

Explore online learning platforms such as Coursera, Udemy, or Khan Academy for courses relevant to your interests. Set up notifications for webinars or podcasts on topics you wish to learn about. Create a digital learning plan to structure your time and resources effectively.

5. Join Learning Communities
Learning communities, such as professional organizations,

study groups, or online forums, offer opportunities for networking, collaboration, and shared learning experiences.

Engaging with learning communities enhances your confidence by connecting you with like-minded individuals and providing support and resources for your learning journey.

Identify relevant learning communities or professional groups related to your interests or field. Actively participate in discussions, attend events, and contribute to group activities. Networking with others can provide new insights and encouragement.

6. Integrate Learning into Daily Life
Incorporating learning into your daily routine helps make continuous growth a manageable and sustainable practice.

Regular learning activities reinforce your commitment to personal development and maintain your confidence in your evolving abilities.

Dedicate specific time slots each day or week for learning activities. This could include reading articles, watching educational videos, or practicing new skills. Even short, consistent periods of learning can lead to significant progress over time.

7. Celebrate Achievements

Recognizing and celebrating your learning achievements acknowledges your progress and reinforces your confidence in your abilities.

Celebrating achievements boosts your self-esteem and encourages a positive attitude towards learning and growth.

Create a "celebration ritual" for acknowledging your learning milestones. This could be as simple as treating yourself to a favorite activity or sharing your achievements with friends or colleagues. Regularly celebrate your progress to stay motivated and positive.

8. Embrace Challenges as Learning Opportunities

Viewing challenges as opportunities for learning rather than obstacles helps you approach difficulties with a growth mindset.

Embracing challenges builds resilience and confidence by demonstrating your ability to overcome obstacles and grow from the experience.

When faced with a challenge, identify the learning opportunities it presents. Reflect on what you can gain from the experience and how it can contribute to your personal or professional growth. Approach challenges with curiosity and a willingness to learn.

9. Practice Self-Discipline and Time Management

Effective self-discipline and time management are essential for balancing learning with other responsibilities and ensuring consistent progress.

Developing self-discipline and managing your time effectively help you stay committed to your learning goals and build confidence through steady progress.

Create a weekly schedule that includes dedicated time for learning activities. Set specific deadlines for achieving learning milestones and hold yourself accountable. Use productivity tools or apps to manage your time and stay organized.

10. Foster a Supportive Learning Environment

A supportive learning environment, whether at home, work, or through online communities, can enhance your learning experience and reinforce your confidence.

A positive and encouraging environment provides motivation and resources, making it easier to stay committed to your learning goals.

Create a dedicated space for learning where you feel comfortable and focused. Surround yourself with supportive individuals who encourage your growth and share your learning interests. Engage in collaborative learning experiences to benefit from different perspectives and insights.

Conclusion

Lifelong learning is a cornerstone of maintaining and growing confidence in a constantly evolving world. By cultivating curiosity, setting learning goals, seeking feedback, leveraging technology, joining learning communities, integrating learning into daily life, celebrating achievements, embracing challenges, practicing self-discipline, and fostering a supportive environment, you can build and sustain your confidence throughout your life. Embrace the journey of continuous growth with enthusiasm and commitment, and let your dedication to learning empower you to navigate new experiences and opportunities with self-assurance and competence. Through lifelong learning, you not only enhance your skills and knowledge but also reinforce your belief in your ability to thrive and succeed.

The Conclusion

CHAPTER FIFTEEN

Live with Confidence, Every Day

Confidence is not a destination but a journey. This final chapter encourages you to integrate confidence-building practices into your daily life. Embrace the call to action to achieve your full potential and live confidently every day.

Confidence is not a static state or a final destination; it is a continuous journey. To truly embody confidence, you must integrate practices and habits into your daily life that reinforce and build upon your self-assurance. This final chapter encourages you to embrace a proactive approach to confidence, providing practical exercises and strategies to help you live confidently every day. By making these practices a part of your routine, you can unlock your full potential and experience a more fulfilling, confident life.

Embracing Daily Confidence Practices
Integrating confidence-building practices into your daily life helps reinforce positive self-beliefs and actions. These practices not only improve your self-esteem but also enhance your interactions, decision-making, and overall well-being.

Benefits of Daily Confidence Practices:
Consistency in Self-Belief:
Regularly engaging in confidence-building activities reinforces a positive self-image and strengthens your belief in your abilities.

Improved Mental Resilience:
Daily practices help you handle challenges and setbacks with greater ease, maintaining a confident attitude even in difficult situations.

Enhanced Self-Awareness:
Consistent reflection and self-assessment improve your understanding of your strengths, areas for growth, and overall self-awareness.

Positive Habit Formation:
Integrating confidence practices into your routine fosters positive habits that contribute to long-term confidence and personal development.

Increased Motivation and Productivity:
Confidence practices boost your motivation and productivity by providing a sense of purpose and direction in your daily activities.

Daily Confidence-Building Exercises

Morning Affirmations
Starting your day with positive affirmations sets a confident tone for the day. Affirmations are powerful

statements that reinforce your self-belief and intentions. Morning affirmations boost your self-esteem, set a positive mindset, and prepare you for a successful day.

Create a list of affirmations that resonate with you, such as "I am capable and confident," or "I embrace challenges with resilience." Each morning, take a few minutes to repeat these affirmations aloud or silently, focusing on their meaning and visualizing a successful day.

Daily Goal Setting

Setting daily goals provides direction and purpose, helping you focus on achievable tasks and celebrate your accomplishments.

Daily goal setting enhances your confidence by giving you clear objectives to work towards and a sense of achievement upon completion.

Each evening, jot down three specific goals for the following day. Ensure these goals are realistic and aligned with your broader objectives. Review your progress at the end of the day and adjust your goals as needed.

Gratitude Practice

Practicing gratitude shifts your focus towards positive aspects of your life, reinforcing a sense of self-worth and confidence.

Gratitude practice improves your overall outlook, reduces stress, and enhances your self-esteem by highlighting the positive aspects of your life.

Each evening, write down three things you are grateful for. Reflect on why these things are significant and how they contribute to your sense of confidence and well-being. Regularly reviewing your gratitude list can provide perspective and boost your mood.

Reflective Journaling
Reflective journaling helps you process your experiences, identify patterns, and reinforce positive self-beliefs.
Journaling enhances self-awareness, supports personal growth, and helps you track your progress in building confidence.
Set aside time each day to journal about your experiences, challenges, and successes. Focus on how you handled situations, what you learned, and how you can continue to grow. Use journaling prompts such as "What went well today?" or "How did I overcome a challenge?"

Confidence-Boosting Activities
Engaging in activities that challenge you and push you out of your comfort zone helps build confidence and resilience. Participating in confidence-boosting activities increases your self-assurance, expands your skill set, and fosters a sense of accomplishment.
Identify activities that stretch your abilities and interests, such as public speaking, learning a new skill, or taking on a leadership role. Commit to engaging in at least one confidence-boosting activity each week and reflect on your experiences afterward.

Mindfulness and Visualization
Mindfulness and visualization techniques help you stay grounded and focused, enhancing your confidence and reducing anxiety.
Mindfulness and visualization improve your ability to manage stress, maintain a positive mindset, and visualize successful outcomes.
Practice mindfulness through deep breathing or meditation

for a few minutes each day. Additionally, spend a few moments visualizing successful scenarios related to your goals. Imagine yourself handling challenges confidently and achieving desired outcomes.

Seek and Provide Feedback

Seeking and providing constructive feedback fosters personal and professional growth, helping you improve and reinforce your confidence.

Feedback provides valuable insights, supports skill development, and enhances your self-awareness and confidence.

Actively seek feedback from peers, mentors, or supervisors on your performance and areas for improvement. Similarly, offer constructive feedback to others in a supportive manner. Use this feedback to set actionable goals and track your progress.

Celebrate Small Wins

Recognizing and celebrating small achievements helps reinforce a sense of accomplishment and boosts your confidence.

Celebrating small wins enhances your motivation, acknowledges your progress, and reinforces your belief in your abilities.

Create a "win jar" where you record your daily or weekly achievements, no matter how small. Periodically review your wins to celebrate your progress and remind yourself of your capabilities.

Maintain a Healthy Lifestyle

A healthy lifestyle, including proper nutrition, exercise, and sleep, supports overall well-being and confidence.

A healthy lifestyle improves your physical and mental health, boosts your energy levels, and enhances your self-esteem.

Incorporate regular exercise into your routine, eat a balanced diet, and prioritize adequate sleep. Set specific health-related goals, such as completing a weekly workout or preparing nutritious meals, and track your progress.

Develop a Growth Mindset

Adopting a growth mindset involves viewing challenges and failures as opportunities for learning and development. A growth mindset encourages resilience, fosters continuous improvement, and supports a confident approach to overcoming obstacles.

When faced with a setback or challenge, reflect on what you can learn from the experience. Focus on the skills you can develop and the opportunities for growth. Remind yourself that failure is a stepping stone to success.

Integrating Confidence Practices into Daily Life

To truly live with confidence every day, it's essential to integrate these practices seamlessly into your routine. Start by identifying which exercises resonate most with you and gradually incorporate them into your daily life. Consistency is key to making these practices habitual and effective.

Steps to Integration:

Create a Routine: Develop a daily or weekly routine that includes the confidence-building exercises you find most beneficial. Set reminders or schedule time in your calendar to ensure you stay consistent.

Track Your Progress: Use a journal or planner to track your

progress and reflect on the impact of these practices on your confidence. Regularly review your achievements and adjust your practices as needed.

Stay Flexible: Be open to adjusting your routine as you discover what works best for you. Experiment with different practices and find a balance that supports your growth and confidence.

Engage with Supportive Networks: Share your confidence-building journey with supportive friends, family, or mentors. Their encouragement and feedback can reinforce your commitment and provide additional motivation.

Conclusion
Living with confidence every day requires a proactive approach to integrating confidence-building practices into your daily life. By embracing morning affirmations, setting daily goals, practicing gratitude, engaging in reflective journaling, participating in confidence-boosting activities, and utilizing mindfulness techniques, you can continuously reinforce and enhance your self-assurance. Seek and provide feedback, celebrate your achievements, maintain a healthy lifestyle, and develop a growth mindset to support your ongoing journey of confidence. As you integrate these practices into your routine, you will unlock your full potential and experience a more fulfilling, confident life. Embrace the journey of daily confidence, and let your commitment to growth and self-belief guide you toward achieving your goals and living your best life.

Enter Caption

Disclaimer

The information provided in this book is intended for educational and informational purposes only. While every effort has been made to ensure the accuracy of the content, the author and publisher make no guarantees regarding the effectiveness or outcomes of the techniques and strategies discussed.

Readers are encouraged to apply their own judgment and consult with appropriate professionals when necessary. The author and publisher are not responsible for any consequences arising from the use or misuse of the information contained herein. Your journey toward personal development is unique, and results may vary.

By reading this book, you acknowledge and agree to these terms.

Feel free to modify it to better fit your style or needs!

How To Contact The Author

Thank you for your interest in connecting! I would love to hear from you. You can reach me through the following channels:

Email: learnwithbhavesh@gmail.com

Social Media: Youtube : Bhavesh Poojari

Instagram:Bhaveshpoojari1

LinkedIn :Bhavesh Poojari

Feel free to share your thoughts, questions, or feedback about the book. Your insights are invaluable, and I appreciate your support on this journey!

Thank You Note

Thank you so much for purchasing this book!

I know you had countless self-help options to choose from, and I am truly grateful that you decided to take a chance on mine. Your support means the world to me!

If you find value in this book, I would be sincerely appreciative if you could take a moment to share it with your friends. Your recommendation could be the spark that helps them achieve their goals and lead happier, more fulfilling lives. They will surely be thankful to you for it, and so will I.

Thank you once again for being a part of this journey. Together, we can inspire positive change!